Lives and Times

Robert Fulton

Jennifer Blizin Gillis

Heinemann Library
Chicago, Illinois

Page layout by Cherylyn Bredemann
Map by John Fleck
Photo research by Alan Gottlieb

Printed and bound in Hong Kong and China by South China Printing Co Ltd

08 07 06 05 04
10 9 8 7 6 5 4 3 2 1

Library of Congress
Cataloging-in-Publication Data
Robert Fulton / Jennifer Blizin Gillis.
ISBN 1-4034-5328-4 (HC), 1-4034-5336-5 (Pbk.)
The Cataloging-in-Publication Data for this title is on file with the Library of Congress.

Acknowledgments
The author and publishers are grateful to the following for permission to reproduce copyright material:
Title page Corbis; icon (steamboat), pp. 6, 21, 25 General Research Division/New York Public Library/Astor Lenox and Tilden Foundations; icon (submarine) Steve Kaufman/Corbis; pp. 4, 5, 7, 26 Bettmann/Corbis; p. 8 The Bridgeman Art Library; p. 9 The New York Historical Society, neg. #1976.14; p. 10 Tate Gallery, London/Art Resource, NY; p. 11 Castle/Devon Mary Evans Picture Library; pp. 12, 14 Mary Evans Picture Library; p. 13 Rare Books and Manuscripts Division/New York Public Library/Astor, Lenox and Tilden Foundations; p. 15 The Bill Douglas Centre/University of Exeter; p. 16 Library of Congress; p. 17 Manuscripts and Archives Division/The New York Public Library/Astor, Lenox and Tilden Foundations; p. 18 The New York Historical Society, neg. # 1876.1; p. 19 Lauros/Giraudon/Bridgeman Art Library; p. 20 Archivo Iconografico, S. A./Corbis; p. 22 Prints and Photographs Division/New York Public Library/Astor, Lenox and Tilden Foundations; p. 24 The New York Historical Society, neg. #1924.7; p. 27 Courtesy of U. S. Naval Institute Photo Archive; p. 28 New York Public Library; p. 29 Gail Mooney/Corbis

Cover photographs by (top left) General Research Division/New York Public Library/Astor Lenox and Tilden Foundations, (bottom left) Corbis, (bottom right) Bettmann/Corbis

The publisher would like to thank Charly Rimsa for her comments in the preparation of this book.

Every effort has been made to contact copyright holders of any material reproduced in this book. Any omissions will be rectified in subsequent printings if notice is given to the publisher.

Some words are shown in bold, **like this.** You can find out what they mean by looking in the glossary.

Contents

Steam Power!

In the early 1800s, there was much open land in the western part of the United States. But it was hard to get to. There were few roads. Robert Fulton thought people could travel there by water.

This **portrait** of Robert Fulton was painted before he became famous.

This is what steamboats looked like in the 1700s.

Robert began **experiments** to make a kind of boat that uses steam to move. Robert made the first large **steamboat** that worked. His invention made it possible for **settlers** to move west.

Early Life

Robert was born in Pennsylvania in 1765. His family lived on a small farm. The land was not good for farming. Soon, the farm failed. The Fulton family had to move away.

Robert spent some of his childhood on this farm.

Robert's father worked as a **tailor** in Lancaster, Pennsylvania. Robert was nine years old when his father died. Robert's mother took care of Robert and his brother and sisters.

In Robert's time, clothes were not made in factories. Tailors made one outfit at a time.

School and Work

Robert's mother sent him to a **tutor** for a while. When he was seventeen, Robert moved to Philadelphia, Pennsylvania. There, he became an **apprentice** to learn how to be a **silversmith.**

Robert would have made things out of silver very much the way this worker is doing.

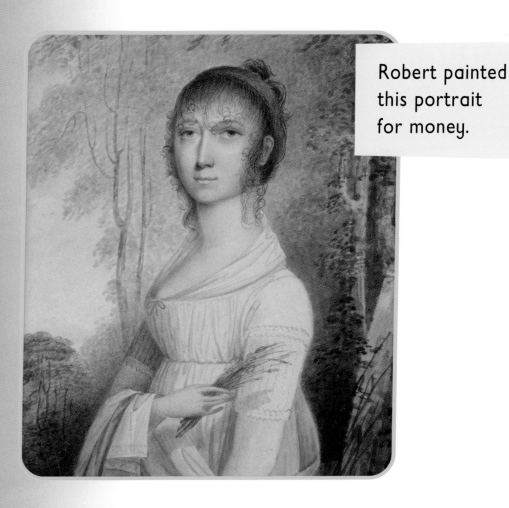

Robert painted this portrait for money.

Robert decided that he wanted to be a painter instead of a silversmith. He started painting people's **portraits.** There were no cameras in the 1700s, so people had their pictures painted by artists.

Living in Britain

London was one of the busiest cities in the world when Robert lived there.

In 1787 Robert went to London. He met a famous painter named Benjamin West. Benjamin helped Robert get painting jobs. Robert was hired to paint the **portrait** of a rich man who lived in Devonshire.

There was beautiful stone called **marble** in Devonshire. Robert watched how hard people worked to carve the stone. He invented a machine that made it easier for them to cut and polish the marble.

Robert lived in this castle in Devonshire for almost two years.

Learning About Canals

The roads in Devonshire were bad. It was hard to move heavy things in wagons. Robert heard about a **canal** that was being built. He thought canals were the best way to move heavy things.

The Bude Canal was built to carry things through Devonshire.

Bude Canal and Harbour

Robert's machine used long ramps to help move boats in and out of the water.

Robert drew plans for a machine that could help move boats through the canals. Robert wrote to President George Washington. He wanted Washington to build canals in the United States.

On to Paris

Robert decided to go to Paris, France. There were many **canals** there. He wanted to talk to more people about his canal ideas. He hoped he could get money to build canals in the United States.

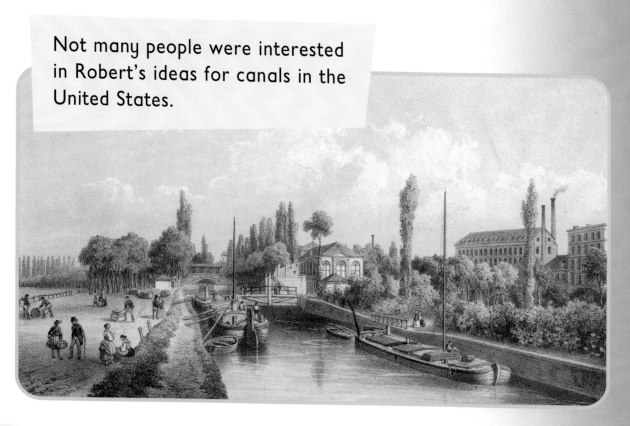

Not many people were interested in Robert's ideas for canals in the United States.

To make money, Robert built a **panorama.** It had a picture on the walls inside. When people stood in the building, it looked like they were seeing Paris from the top of a mountain.

This is a panorama from 1792. People paid about 33 cents to go inside Robert's panorama, or about $5.00 in today's money.

The *Nautilus*

In 1800 Robert built a **submarine** called the *Nautilus*. Above water, it looked like a sailboat. People were amazed that the *Nautilus* could stay underwater for several hours.

Robert planned for the *Nautilus* to go underneath ships and attack them with **torpedoes.**

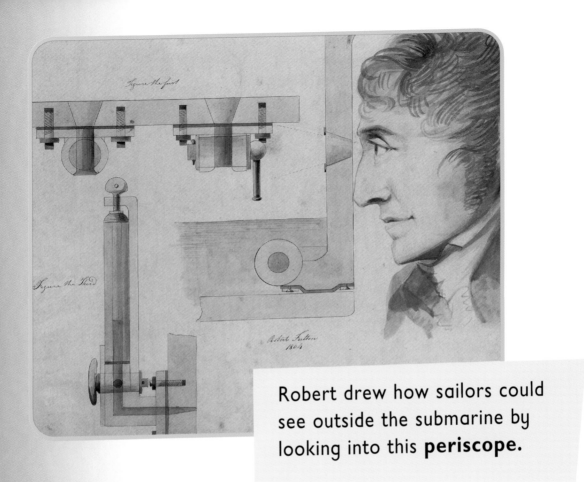

Robert drew how sailors could see outside the submarine by looking into this **periscope.**

Robert tried to sell his submarine to the French **government.** In 1801 the government agreed to buy it. But Robert said the submarine was worn out. He sold it to people one piece at a time.

Clermont 1807

The Steamboat Begins

Robert Livingston became Robert's partner in building steamboats.

Many people heard about Robert's **submarine.** One of them was Robert Livingston. Livingston was trying to build a **steamboat** that could carry passengers from New York City to Albany on the Hudson River.

Robert built a **model** boat. It had a steam engine that turned wheels on the side. Robert tested the model in a river. It worked! He left France to build a real steamboat in the United States.

This old painting shows a steamboat on the Seine River in Paris, France.

Fulton's Folly

Robert sailed to New York. He went to work building a new **steamboat.** People thought it would never work. They called it Fulton's "folly," or a silly idea. No one had made a steamboat that did not sink.

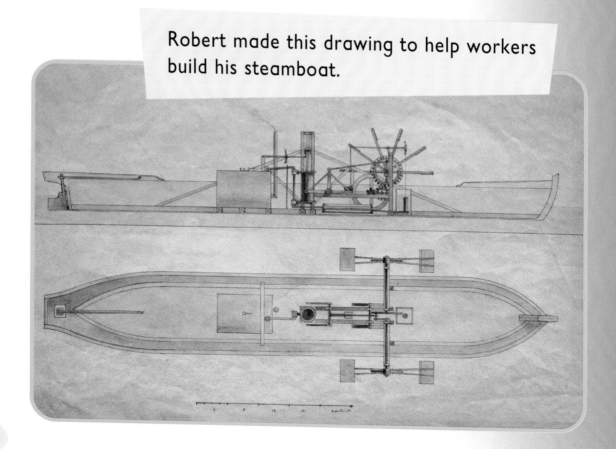

Robert made this drawing to help workers build his steamboat.

The steamboat's engine turned the paddlewheels. The paddlewheels pushed against the water to make the boat move.

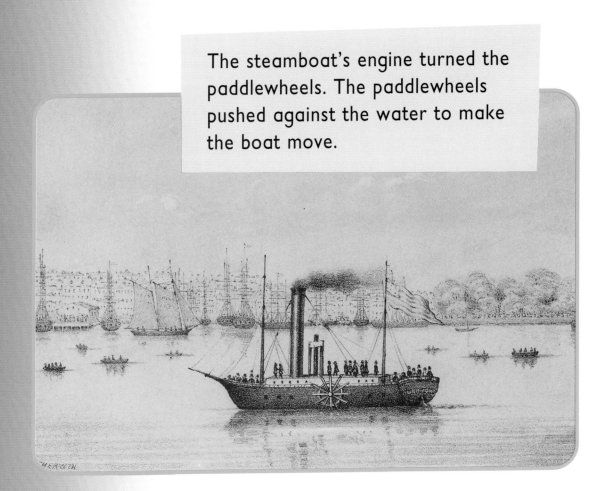

This steamboat had paddlewheels, too. It was long and thin with square sides. A huge steam engine sat in the middle of the boat. There were sails, too, in case the engine stopped working.

The Sea Monster

On August 17, 1807, people along the Hudson River saw something strange chug by. So much smoke was coming from it that people thought it was on fire. It was so noisy people thought it was a monster.

The first passengers on the *North River* paid $7 each, or about $102 today, to go from Albany to New York City.

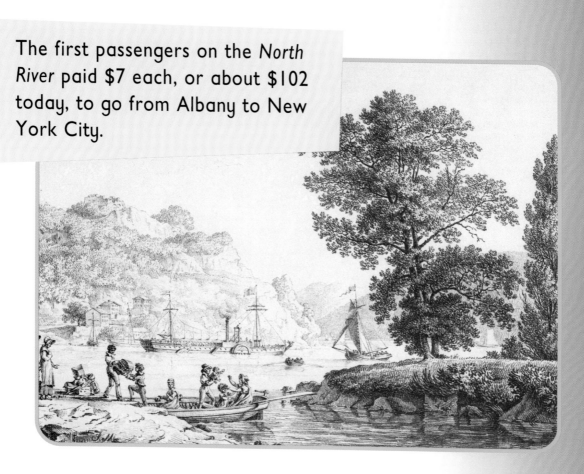

Albany is the **capital** of New York State. People from New York needed a way to travel there quickly and safely.

The monster was Robert Fulton's **steamboat,** the *North River!* It went from New York City to Albany in 32 hours. It took sailing ships 4 days to make the same trip.

Marriage and Success

While he was building the *North River*, Robert met Robert Livingston's niece, Harriet. She was a painter and a musician. In 1808 Robert married Harriet. They had four children together.

Robert painted this **portrait** of his wife Harriet in 1810.

Robert made his steamboats better and better. Some had beds for passengers, fancy carpets, and curtains inside.

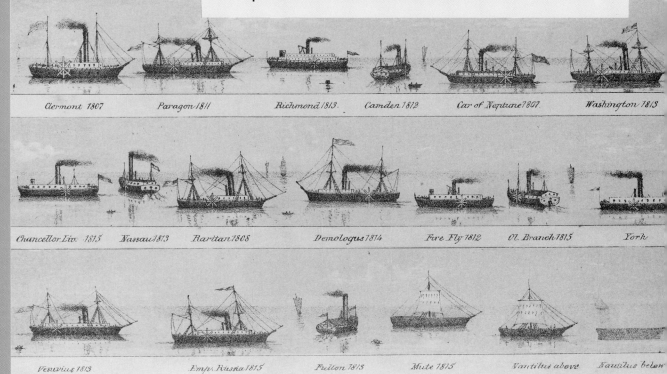

Clermont 1807   Paragon 1811   Richmond 1813   Camden 1812   Car of Neptune 1807   Washington 1813

Chancellor Liv. 1815   Nassau 1813   Raritan 1808   Demologus 1814   Fire Fly 1812   Ol. Branch 1815   York

Vesuvius 1813   Empr. Russia 1815   Fulton 1813   Mute 1815   Nautilus above   Nautilus below

The *North River* was a success. In the next four years, Robert built other **steamboats.** Soon, he and his **business partner** had steamboats on many rivers, including the Mississippi River.

War!

In 1814 the United States and Great Britain were at war. Robert returned to his **experiments** with **submarines.** When the British set fire to Washington, D.C., Robert sent some **torpedoes** to a fort that was under attack.

The British set fire to the U.S. Capitol and the White House during the War of 1812.

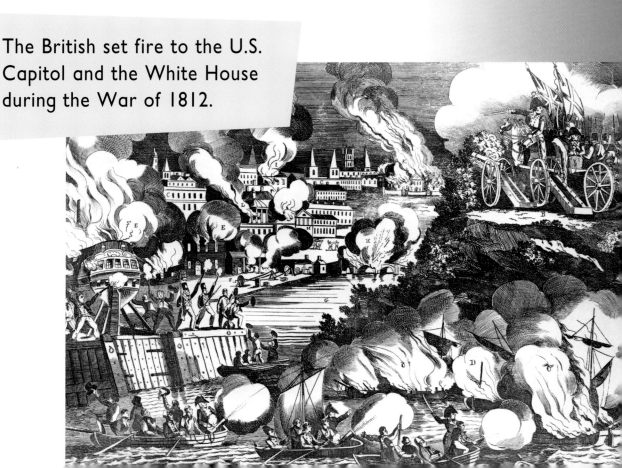

The U.S. government wanted the *Fulton I* to float in New York Harbor and shoot at British ships.

The U.S. **government** gave Robert money to build a warship. Robert built a huge **steamboat** called the *Fulton I.* It had 30 **cannons** on it.

Lifelong Inventor

During his lifetime, Robert got nine **patents** for things he invented.

Robert worked hard throughout his life. After he built the *North River*, Robert built sixteen more **steamboats.** He also kept painting and drawing.

When he was 49 years old, Robert caught a cold. He became very sick. Robert died in 1815.

Robert was buried at Trinity Church in New York City.

Fact File

- Robert was a poor speller all his life. His letters were full of spelling mistakes.

- Robert's **steamboat** the *North River* later came to be known as the *Clermont*. This was the name of the place where Robert's **business partner** Robert Livingston lived.

- Robert had four children: a boy named Robert and three girls named Julia, Cornelia, and Mary.

Timeline

1765	Robert Fulton is born on November 14.
1782	Robert becomes an **apprentice** to a **silversmith** in Philadelphia.
1796	Robert publishes a book on **canal** design and improvements.
1799	Robert opens his **panorama** in Paris.
1800	Robert tests his first **submarine,** the *Nautilus,* in Paris.
1802	Robert begins working on his first steamboat.
1807	The *North River* (later called the *Clermont*) makes first trip carrying passengers on August 17.
1808	Robert marries Harriet Livingston.
1814	Robert builds the warship *Fulton I.*
1815	Robert dies on February 24.

Glossary

apprentice   person who learns a job by working with someone who is an expert

business partner   person who works with someone else to run a business

canal   human-made river that is like a highway used by boats to carry people and things from one place to another

cannon   huge gun that shoots large balls of heavy metal

capital   important city where the government is located

experiment   test that is done to discover or prove something

government   group of people who rule a country

marble   strong, smooth stone that can be carved into different shapes

model   small copy of a thing

panorama   circular painting that shows a view of a place from every direction

patent   legal paper given to a person that says he or she is the only person allowed to make a certain invention unless special permission is given

periscope   tool that helps people in a submarine see above the water

portrait   painting or drawing of a person

settler   person who moves from one place to live in another place

silversmith   person who makes things out of silver, such as jewelry or plates

steamboat   boat that uses a steam engine to turn large wheels that push against the water to make the boat move

submarine   ship that can move underwater

tailor   person who earns money by making clothing

torpedo   weapon that blows up ships

tutor   teacher who gives lessons at home

Clermont 1807

More Books to Read

An older reader can help you with these books:

Ford, Carin T. *Robert Fulton: The Steamboat Man.* Berkeley Heights, N.J.: Enslow, 2004.

Rosenberg, Pam. *Robert Fulton.* Chanhassen, Minn.: Child's World, 2003.

Schaefer, Lola M. *Robert Fulton.* Mankato, Minn.: Capstone Press, 2000.

Index